Evolution Revolution

By

Nadja

NadjaMedia.com

Nadja Media
530 Los Angeles Ave., Suite 115
Moorpark, California 93021

Cover art by Katrina Joyner

ISBN-10: 1942057075
ISBN-13: 978-1-942057-07-9

Copyright © 2011 by Nadja.

All rights reserved. No part of this book may be reproduced by any mechanical, photographic, or electronic process, or in the form of a phonographic recording; nor may it be stored in a retrieval system, transmitted, or otherwise be copied for public or private use—other than for "fair use" as brief quotations embodied in articles and reviews—without prior written permission of the publisher.

This is a work of fiction. Names, characters, places, and incidents either are a product of the author's imagination or are used fictitiously, and any resemblance to actual persons, living or dead, business establishments, events, or locales is entirely coincidental. No liability is assumed for damages resulting from the use of or misinterpretation of information contained herein. The information is meant as a guideline only and to help Humanity better reflect upon themselves, where they have been, where they are now, and where they potentially may be going. The author is not a medical doctor and does not give medical advice. If you are having problems you need to consult with a medical professional or a certified counselor. Nadja never advocates the use of violence in any form.

Dedication

For those who are seeking change and transformation to become all they were meant to be and to take their rightful place in the New Earth.

— Nadja

Acknowledgments

With gratitude for the Spark of God which has been bestowed upon all of us.

Introduction

Are you concerned or fearful about the future? You are here to play an important part in this Time of Great Change. Find out how you can participate. Read this and you will be filled with hope, excitement, and knowledge as each day unfolds. This book contains embedded energy transmissions for awakening.

Evolution Revolution

by
Nadja

YOU CAME TO PLAY YOUR PART

Look up and live

A revolution's going on

It's spreading everywhere

Come along and sing your song

We are all changing

We are growing and evolving

There's a worldwide revolution

You are needed for resolving

You Came To Play Your Part

The Planet's in trouble

Your help is needed badly

The situation's very serious

And it might end sadly

The greatest revolution

Is right inside of you

Daily count your blessings

And your mind will renew

YOU CAME TO PLAY YOUR PART

Nothing to be thankful for?

What about the sky

The stars and the sun

And the birds that fly by?

The flowers, the trees

Your body, the Earth

The chance to laugh and cry

Since the day of your birth?

There's a revolution

Look up and live

Say Yes to life

Find out what you can give

We have no time to waste

You came to play your part

Your help is badly needed

Learn to live from your heart

YOU CAME TO PLAY YOUR PART

Don't entertain the negative

The ugly and the Dark

These thoughts stop you

From playing your true part

Your life may be hard

Filled with sadness and pain

But by daily counting blessings

You have everything to gain

You Came To Play Your Part

You can crawl out

From that deeply hidden cave

Where it's dark, cold, and lonely

Seek the Light and be brave

Hurt grows anger

Anger grows hate

This can mess up your life

And darken your fate

YOU CAME TO PLAY YOUR PART

Listen to your anger

Let it talk to you

Find out where it comes from

Release and renew

Watch what you're thinking

Don't believe your mind

It's the Big Trickster

And will keep you blind

YOU CAME TO PLAY YOUR PART

What is your talent?

You were born with one or more

Seek it out, develop it

Then you will score

Change your head

Move from mind to heart

This is work needed

To play your true part

Look up and live

Praise God above

Cast your cares on Him

And feel His love

He loves you so much

How can you measure?

He buried deep within you

His priceless treasure

Get really quiet

Away from friends and noise

In gratitude and praise

Listen to His Voice

You may not hear it

On your first try

But do this daily

And someday by and by

You will hear that small voice

From down deep within

It will guide you truly

Through the thick and the thin

You will learn how to love

Yourself and others

The world all around you

Your sisters and brothers

Don'tcha know

We are all One

The world and its people

Mother Nature and the Sun

Be still and seek

The God within

By doing this daily

You will change where you've been

You Came To Play Your Part

Look around you

As you work at praise

The world seems to change

Vibrations you help raise

Your life gets better

More Light comes in

You send more Light out

From deep down within

Get your act together

Clean up your mess

Do your inside Work

Let go of stress

Addictions and distractions

Will just hold you back

From knowing who you are

And keep you off track

You Came To Play Your Part

They are there to mislead you

Placed there by the Dark

So you can't focus

On playing your true part

Now is the time

To look up and live

Free your soul

And learn how to give

Let go of the past

It is dead

Live moment to moment

In the Light instead

Be happy, find joy

Welcome each day

Greet everyone you see

This is the way

Watch the world change

When you live like this

It'll transform before you

And you will not miss

Being unhappy and sad

As you used to be

But now you are free

To really truly See

You are worthy

You are loved

This is the Gift

Given from Above

Join with the ones

Who are now awake

They are giving their Light

A new world to make

Clean yourself up first

Then your neighborhood

On to the world

Spread out the Good

Don't count on others

Be your own best friend

Just rely on yourself

Don't attack but defend

Don't be a follower

Think for yourself

Go deep within

Find the True Wealth

Become a leader

Show the Way

To a positive life

And a Brand New Day

Be the change

You would like to see

To heal Mother Earth

Every person and tree

This beats negativity

And ending up dead

By saying Yes to Life

And blooming instead

You Came To Play Your Part

Come out of the shadows

Live in the Light

Play your true part

Both day and night

Look deep within

Surrender, let go

Let the Light in

Go with its flow

You Came To Play Your Part

We have no time to waste

You came to play your part

Your help is needed badly

Learn to live from your heart

Look up and live

A revolution's going on

It's spreading everywhere

Come along and sing your song

Final Words

"What lies behind us and what lies before us are tiny matters compared to what lies within us."

— Ralph Waldo Emerson

Resources

Helpguide.org—Free resources to help you resolve mental and emotional health issues. Includes hotlines and support groups. Helps you help yourself and others.

FoodBabe.com

Mercola.com

NaturalNews.com

Bioneers.org

WestonPrice.org

NextWorldTV.com

CalixtoSuarez.com

Crimes Against Nature by Robert F. Kennedy

Cosmic Ordering Made Easier by Ellen Watts

M. T. Keshe

Santos Bonacci

Dr. Masaru Emoto

Scott Werner, M.D.

Vandana Shiva

Masanobu Fukuoka

Chunyi Lin

Susun Weed

Tusli Gabbard

John Hagelin, Ph.D.

Paul Stamets

Buckmaster Fuller

David Wilcock

Matt Kahn

Lynn Waldrop

John Newton

Christel Hughes

Debora Wayne

Tarek Bibi

Lanna Spencer

Sophia Zoe

Magenta Pixie

Jo Dunning

Lisa Transcendence Brown

Julie Renee

Eckhart Tolle

Neale Donald Walsch

Stacey Mayo

Dorian Light

Lottie Cooper

Andie DePass

Judy Cali

Marianne Williamson

Dr. Madlena Kantscheff

Dipal Shah

Peta Amber Lynne

Anamika

Sarah Lynn Kennedy

Emmanuel Dagher

Jenny Ngo

Jarrad Hewett

Tamra Oviatt

Cathy Hohmeyer

Morry Zelcovitch

Rassouli

Akiane Kramarik

SARK

Shiloh Sophia

Aviva Gold

Ho'oponopono

The Emotion Code by Bradley Nelson

Emotional Freedom Technique (EFT)

Acim.org

Wopg.org

BirthingAndRebirthing.com

YouWealthRevolution.com

FromHeartacheToJoy.com

AcousticHealth.com

GalacticConnection.com

Chanchka.com

GeoEngineeringWatch.org

RingingCedars.com

TED.com

TheGrowNetwork.com

NotesFromTheUniverse.com

Homeopathic Cell Salts

OptimumHealthInstitute.com

NewPhoenixRising.com

About the Author

After working many years in the public sector Nadja is reinventing herself as an artist and writer. She has an eclectic background. Her joys include adventuring on the Open Road, dancing, cooking, being in nature, writing and painting. She is also interested in natural building, organic gardening, alternative health, life-long learning, travel, and living moment to moment. Nadja writes for the conscious community and people who are interested in healing, meditation, transformation, ascension, and the New Earth. This includes highly sensitive people, Starseeds, Indigos, empaths, Light Workers, energy healers, artists, visionaries, and those in recovery and discovery.

Also by Nadja

Soft-cover books, eBooks, MP3s, and CDs, Smashwords, Amazon, Kindle, CreateSpace, CDBaby, iTunes, YouTube, and your local bookstore by request.

River of Living Light

Evolution Revolution

Random Thoughts and Poems

Hopi Blue Corn

El Maiz Azul de los Hopis

Visionary Tales for the New Earth

Color Me Bright Coloring Book

Blue Sky

Ascension Codes

Raps, Chants, and Rants

Women's Power Awakened

Ozzengoggle Poems

From the City of Shem

You Are Not Alone

Family Secrets

Flying Heart

Bullies

www.ingramcontent.com/pod-product-compliance
Lightning Source LLC
Chambersburg PA
CBHW070800050426
42452CB00012B/2430